June 1

P9-DWZ-117

Dear Roseanne,

I am so sorry for your loss. You had such a long time together which makes the loss wider.

I'm glad you had so many good years together.

Stan was a good match for you and I assume was good to you.

I wish you wellness as you walk through this troubled time.

Love,
your friend
Suzi Lindley

new phone # - cards old. 707 8(3 0138

THE AWAKENED HEART

*Meditations on Finding Harmony
in a Changing World*

The Inner Light Series

The Inner Light Series is a collection of spiritual works that strive to inspire and illuminate the quest of a new generation of seekers. While the wisdom these books contain is classic, the language and metaphor through which it is expressed are contemporary and accessible to a wide and growing audience. We hope these books will become treasured companions on your unfolding journey of spirit.

Titles in the Series

The Laws of Spirit by Dan Millman
The Alchemy of Prayer by Terry Lynn Taylor
The Awakened Heart by John Robbins and Ann Mortifee

THE AWAKENED HEART

*Meditations on Finding Harmony
in a Changing World*

John Robbins
&
Ann Mortifee

H J KRAMER
TIBURON, CALIFORNIA

H J Kramer Inc
P.O. Box 1082
Tiburon, CA 94920

Editor: Nancy Grimley Carleton
Editorial Assistant: Claudette Charbonneau
Cover Design: Jim Marin/Marin Graphic Services
Composition: Classic Typography
Book Production: Schuettge & Carleton
Manufactured in the United States of America.
10 9 8 7 6 5 4 3 2 1

Library of Congress Cataloging-in-Publication Data
Robbins, John.
  The awakened heart : meditations on finding harmony in a
changing world / John Robbins and Ann Mortifee.
    p. cm.
  Rev. ed. of: In search of balance. 1991.
  ISBN 0-915811-74-X
  I. Meditations. I. Mortifee, Ann, 1947–   . II. Robbins, John.
In search of balance. III. Title.
BL624.2.R62 1997
299'.93–dc21   96-40536
                                                         CIP

To Devon and Ocean,
our sons

To Our Readers

The books we publish
are our contribution to
an emerging world based on
cooperation rather than on competition,
on affirmation of the human spirit rather
than on self-doubt, and on the certainty
that all humanity is connected.
Our goal is to touch as many
lives as possible with a
message of hope for
a better world.

Hal and Linda Kramer, Publishers

Contents

Introduction

Ann and John: We were both born in 1947, just after World War II. It was a time when a whole raft of beings was being born onto the planet, entering a situation unlike anything ever known before in human history. The use of the atomic bombs in Hiroshima and Nagasaki, coupled with the revelation of what had occurred in Germany, shook the human spirit to its very roots.

All around the world, the questions echoed: "How could this have happened? What must we do to insure that it will never happen again?" It was into these questions that so many of us were born. And these questions have shaped much of what has occurred in the last few decades.

Some of us said, "We must arm ourselves; we must grow more powerful than the enemy. We must develop our technology, make ourselves impermeable. We must build our physical, ideological, and financial fortresses so that when the inevitable comes we will be prepared."

Others of us said, "We must grow in understanding. We must discover more about ourselves and about our unconscious motivations and possibilities. We must mature in consciousness so that we can meet our intellectual and scientific advancements with a wisdom that is equal to the power we are unleashing."

And still others of us said nothing, being either overwhelmed by or unaware of the immense changes brewing and escalating with each passing year.

In every moment of history, circumstances arise that stimulate and awaken the evolution of humankind. Our time is no exception. A collective inner awareness is forming out of our fundamental instinct for survival. This instinct tells us that, in a nuclear age, war is no longer a viable option for survival. It tells us that with the pain and suffering that are accompanying the rapid growth in population, and with the staggering harm being done to our home, our environment, we can no longer remain estranged from the Earth. Our survival, in fact, depends upon our learning to live consciously in harmony with the delicate nuances and balances of nature's intricate life patterns.

At this very moment, something is arising from the collective unconscious in response to these difficulties and predicaments. Something is taking shape that is as powerful in its own way as are the nuclear weapons and the overwhelming social and environmental realities we face.

Many of us are feeling a deep urge, a prompting from within, that is impelling us to reconnect with the essential Spirit at the core of Creation. We are feeling it in different ways, we are calling it by different names, but ultimately it is the same urge that has called humankind forward since the beginning of time.

John: One of my earliest memories is waiting at night for my father to come home from work, listening for the sound of his car entering the driveway. He often brought ice cream home with him. And it was no wonder, for he and my uncle were the founders of the Baskin-Robbins ice cream company.

As his only son, it was expected that I would follow in his footsteps. From my earliest childhood, I was groomed to run what has become the largest ice cream company in the world.

But something was rising up inside of me saying that this was not my direction. I entered my teenage years and early adulthood in the 1960s. It was a time of tremendous upheaval in North America. A war was being fought that many of us felt was wrong, and a nuclear shadow was looming ominously over our lives. Consciousness was growing about the damage being done to the planetary life-support systems. And the sense of family and community was breaking down through the relentless American drive toward wealth and power.

The generation before mine had lived through the Great Depression and World War II. For them, the pursuit of material security was more than a desire; it was a need. Yet for my generation, something else was calling.

I still remember where I was and how devastated I felt when I first learned that President Kennedy had been assassinated. A couple of years later, watching reports on television of the civil rights movement in the South, I knew I had to go there and be a part of the struggle for human justice. In the summer of 1965, when I was seventeen, I got on a bus headed for Birmingham, Alabama.

I was deeply affected by the example of Dr. Martin Luther King, Jr., and in the following years I joined with him in marching to protest both racism and U.S. involvement in the Vietnam War. King's message of nonviolence, and the powerful force of love that illumined his life, shone for me like a beacon of promise. When he was assassinated, I felt as though a great hole had been punched in my heart.

I chose to follow my conscience, leaving Baskin-Robbins and forgoing any dependence I might have had on my family's money. I chose to venture into a life that would enable me to discover my own values, and to live by my own instincts and powers.

I moved to a tiny island off the coast of British Columbia with my wife, Deo. There I cleared land, built a log cabin, and began to inquire how I might deepen my ability to understand myself and find my connection with the world. Deo and I grew virtually all our own food, and we managed to live on less than five hundred dollars a year. Such a basic and simple life was the only way I knew at the time to attune myself, to heal, and to try to bring my life into alignment with something for which I was still seeking. This phase of my life taught me much about

4

the beauty of simplicity, and the growth that comes with a clarity of purpose.

I hungered for a way of life that could bring both inner and outer peace. I became a psychotherapist, continued to study meditation, yoga, and other forms of healing, and ran a small growth center in British Columbia called the Rising Spirit Center.

On a journey to India, I was affected as deeply by the poverty, squalor, and environmental deterioration that I encountered as I was by the messages of the wisdom traditions and spiritual teachers. I was beginning to realize that to be whole I not only had to face my own pain and shadow, but I also needed to respond with my life to the anguish of our planet and the suffering of its people. Like many of my generation, I was beginning to sense that the quest for personal enlightenment and the work for social justice were inseparable.

Soon thereafter, I moved back to California, wrote the book *Diet for a New America*, and founded the nonprofit organization EarthSave, which promotes the creation of a sane, ethical, and sustainable society by undertaking purposeful nonviolent action on behalf of human and planetary health.

Over the years, I have been involved in a wide range of environmental, public health, and social policy issues. Countless times, I've seen the results that develop from the ways different people express themselves. Even when our efforts to help one another and to improve conditions are well-intentioned, they are often futile when we are beset by unresolved personal issues and anxieties. The most fruitful actions are those we undertake when we are centered in our essence, when we are focused by our passion, when our actions are guided by a sense of spiritual direction.

In today's world, inner peace may be more than a pleasure and a source of personal freedom. It may be the very precondition for effective action and survival.

As I have traveled the country in the last few years, speaking with many tens of thousands of people, I have sensed huge forces stirring and beginning to awaken. Out of the stresses of our age, new human powers are emerging. Everywhere I go, I meet people who want to be fully well, who are tired of feeling overwhelmed, and who are yearning to take charge of their lives. Everywhere there are people who are reclaiming the ability to follow the guidance of their inner wisdom, who are finding their passion and responding to it. A power emerging from our collective roots is calling many of us forward, urging us to acknowledge the inner self in a new way, to take more personal and interpersonal responsibility, and to make our lives authentic statements of who we are.

A few years ago, I began to write about some of the concerns and issues that many of us are facing. After working on the project for a while, though, I reached an impasse. The book was not yet what it should be, but I had not the slightest clue how to move it forward.

It was then that I met a woman named Ann Mortifee.

At the time, I knew that Ann was a successful composer and vocal artist whose voice had a remarkable ability to bring forth deep feelings, and whose albums had been a source of pleasure and inspiration to millions. When I first met her, a sense of recognition came over me like a sudden shaft of light. Although I knew next to nothing about her personally, I felt a wonderfully refreshing sense of connection, and I sensed that I could entrust her with the project. Quite clearly, an inner voice said, "She is the person to take the book the next step."

As it has turned out, *The Awakened Heart* is truly an expression of the mingling of our spirits.

Ann: I was born in South Africa on a large and beautiful sugarcane farm in Zululand. Some of my earliest recollections are of the mystery of that land, of the magnificent and primal music I would hear from my bed in the nighttime, and of an inner confusion South Africa bred with its separation of peoples.

I can still remember a moment when I stood on the veranda of our white house on the hill and wondered why I had been born to my parents, and not to the people in the small mud and thatch huts who lived in the valley below. Why was it the black farm workers, and not I, who lined up every Thursday with an old sack or a rusted-out tin can to get a portion of mealie corn, while I, and not they, always had marmalade and finger biscuits and fine china on the table? Questions like this plagued me, opened me, and drew me into a longing for understanding.

My family moved to Canada. For a time, I looked to organized religions for understanding, for a sense of order and value in the face of the confusion and turmoil I felt and saw all around me. The example of Christ's love awoke a deep and passionate longing in me. I wanted to be able to use my life in order to love as he did, unconditionally, without fear or judgment. The love of which Christ spoke was inclusive; it welcomed us all. But organized religions seemed to be exclusive and to breed more separation. They did not satisfy the desire that had been born in me in South Africa—the desire that all be cherished, that none be abandoned.

Like John, I was profoundly affected by the events of the 1960s. I was fifteen when a friend gave me her old guitar and I discovered the wonder of music. In the years that followed, I wrote songs, ballets, film scores, musicals, and poems. My career was on the ascendant when I came to a choice point. It was 1976, and I had a major contract with EMI Records in London and a world tour in the offing. Yet I felt progressively more uncomfortable and confused about where that path would lead. I knew that my life would become a whirlwind of activity, that I

8

would be out in the public eye so much that I would not have time to grow inwardly. I yearned for something intangible, something that still remained unknown to me.

I left everything to travel for a few years. For a year, I lived in Beirut. I remember standing on a balcony there, watching a woman being beaten and dragged into a car, and the car speeding off. I remember being in a store buying groceries when midway through shopping I had an insistent feeling to go to another shop a few doors down the road and buy my bread. I left a half-full basket of food and walked out onto the street. Within moments, a bomb went off in the store where I had been shopping, killing everyone in it. I remember walking through a bombed-out area of the city when a man suddenly pushed a gun into my cheek and demanded that I get into his car. Though I managed somehow to emerge unscathed, these kinds of experiences took the questions with which I had been living to a deeper level. Where was the love that could heal such violence? What must I do to grow in wisdom so that I could find harmony, peace, and meaning in a world of such paradox?

I left Beirut and went to India, a country whose spiritual richness had always spoken to me, eventually ending up in Calcutta with Mother Teresa and her co-workers. In Mother Teresa, I saw the action of a love that is always expanding to include even the most distressed, a love that crosses over boundaries, that flows into people, touching them, healing them. Through her, I came to sense that it is not what we do or even what we believe that causes love to flower, but who we are in our essential self.

When I returned home to Canada and began my career anew, it was with a deeper commitment than ever before. There were years of recording and performing the songs and music and feelings that had been born during my travels; of concerts and tours, albums and adventures. And then, once again, a feeling came over me to withdraw from public life and to move inward.

At this time, Jack Schwarz invited me to teach with him at a conference on mind-body healing at his Aletheia Center in Ashland, Oregon. Another one of the presenters was to be a man named John Robbins. When I first saw John's picture, I experienced a shock of inner recognition, and a deep feeling that I had always known and cared for him.

At the conference, I was to speak about how sound and the ability to release the inner voice affects our health and well-being. John was talking on how the commitment to personal health affects the health of our environment. As I was moving away from a life in the spotlight, John was moving into one, due to the impact of his magnificent book *Diet for a New America*.

There was a remarkably comfortable and natural connection between us. Perhaps this is always the way with our deepest friends. As someone once said, "Friends are not made; they are recognized."

Shortly thereafter, I had a dream. In the dream, I am walking down an aisle in an ancient library. There seem to be an infinite number of beautifully bound books reaching beyond sight in every direction. In the far distance, I see a man walking toward me. I walk past pillars carved with archetypal symbols and animal figures, with a feeling that I am looking for a specific book. I am concentrating on my search when suddenly I know that I have found it! It is a huge book, much too large for one person to hold. As I reach for it, the hand of another person appears and takes hold of the book with me. It is the hand of the man who had been walking toward me. The man is John.

Together, we lift the book out, each of us holding half of it as we open it. There on the page before us, we see a beautiful picture of a road winding off into the infinite horizon.

Some days later, when John asked me to have a look at a book he was writing, it seemed altogether easy for me to begin.

John and Ann: What follows are heart thoughts, meditations on some of the basic human realities that many seekers today experience. We have written *The Awakened Heart* to discover and support the longings so many of us feel to bring our lives into harmony with deeper truths, to move toward a way of life illumined by respect for the self and for all Creation. It is inspired by the common human hunger to use our lives to bring more love and beauty into the world.

We hope that *The Awakened Heart* will be for you as it has been for us — a stepping-stone over which you walk toward your inner knowing and fulfillment.

PART ONE

THE DEEPEST URGE
OF THE UNIVERSE

Responding to the Call of Love

The Many Hungers

*T*here are many forms of hunger. There is the hunger for food, and there is the hunger for love, for purpose, for truth. There is the hunger for health, for happiness. There is the hunger for companionship, for inner peace, for the sense that we belong. There is the hunger for laughter, and there is the hunger for God.

The hungers that live in the human heart are part of the kinship that threads us all together. We are interdependent beings with a profound need both to give and to receive from one another. For what one of us is lacking, another has in abundance, whether that be a bowl of rice, a skill, a wisdom, a capacity for joy, a knowledge, or a courageous heart. Our urges and our gifts, our longings and our offerings, are all needed and are all indispensable.

When we share the particular gifts that we have been given, we free our life force from its cage of separation. If we were born with a song in our heart, then we must sing it; if there is a vision in our soul, then we must live it. When we express fully all that we are, we participate in the flow of life. We are not meant to sit on the sideline, passively watching others live. We are meant to be vehicles through which our spirits can flow outward to life.

If we are moved by the plight of people who are starving for food, it is because they are a reflection of our own need. They are a reminder not only of that part of us that is hungry, but also of that part of us that needs to give in order to be whole.

Kinship With Life

When we open to ourselves, our lives, and our Earth as sacred, something changes. When we allow the spirit of the Earth to touch us, when we live in contact with the trees, the clouds, the moon, and the soil, when we know that the animals and plants and rocks are our neighbors, then something precious begins to awaken. The forests become cathedrals, and the birds singing in the trees become choirs. We experience all forms of life as part of a great fellowship, and we begin to realize what a tremendous privilege and joy it is to be able to live harmoniously with the whole fabric of Creation.

Today's Tidings

*I*ncreasing numbers of us are sensing a new potential for our lives as a yearning that cannot be denied. It may sometimes seem like an overwhelming burden to keep pace with this new awakening, for living our lives today takes extraordinary attention, courage, and willingness. There are few signposts to point the way. There are few established gauges to measure whether we are doing well or not.

Everything is being rearranged. The assumptions by which we have historically defined ourselves and made sense of the world can no longer provide the same sense of identity and security. Each one of us is experiencing this upheaval in a unique and personal way.

All over the Earth, there are people of all religions, of all cultures, from the most indigenous to the most technological, who are today praying, loving, learning, giving, and listening for guidance. We don't often hear about this in the news, but increasing numbers of us, in our own ways, are working to cooperate with this miraculous unfolding.

Just as a mountain meadow comes alive with many different flowers as the spring sun warms the soil, so the collective consciousness is blossoming in many new forms.

These are the extraordinary tidings of our day.

The New Consciousness

*A*s a new kind of consciousness is being birthed within humankind, we must go through great labor pains to bring forth the new life. We experience these labor contractions as disturbances — outwardly as the stresses we have placed on the environment, and as political, social, and cultural unrest; inwardly, as the pressure to move forward into a world of greater love and health.

We are not passive beings, pressed toward awakening by forces outside us. Our deepest instincts for survival and growth have called this movement, this time in history, into being.

Seeking Inner Harmony

We are both material and spiritual animals, simultaneously pulled by gravity toward the Earth, and by an upward force toward the heavens. We are drawn outward into the world, and at the same time inward to the core of Being.

In one area of our life, we may feel capable, clear, and uplifted; yet in another area we may feel inadequate and unable to cope. At one moment, we may be whole and strong, and at the next moment confused and self-conscious.

Faced with such a contrast in levels of mastery, it is natural that at times we feel torn, out of balance, suspended between heaven and Earth. Yet even when we are confused, there are healing forces at work in our psyches deeper than the conscious mind can perceive.

The balance we seek is not a fixed stability, but a flexible learning process that deepens our ability to sense and live in harmony with a power greater than ourselves, and to bring that harmony into every aspect and moment of our lives.

Choosing What to Believe

When we live believing that life is meaningless, our experience of ourselves becomes less loving, less joyful, less alive. Our bodies feel less vital. Our attitude has a dampening effect on those around us, and we feel robbed of our sense of purpose and pleasure.

If, on the other hand, we live believing that our every thought, word, and deed does in fact make a difference, then our lives become touched by the extraordinary. We have more health, joy, and laughter. We feel brighter, more connected, and others feel more enriched in our company.

When we choose to live as if our lives are linked with the destiny of the entire planet, we weave ourselves back into the web of creation. The threads that unite us are woven by our sense of self-worth, and tied together by the love that finds something worthy and precious in all beings and things.

Acceptance and Love

*A*t the center of all life, there is love. Love is the deepest urge of the universe. Love keeps all of life moving toward greater and richer fullness. Love calls all of life toward peace and harmony, as well as toward change and upheaval.

Love does not exclude anything or anyone from the bounty of her adoration.

And so when we ask "How can I become a vessel for unconditional love?" what we are actually asking is "How can I accept all of life as worthy? How can I give my deepest approval to all beings and all things at all times? How can I open my heart to each experience without judgment or resistance, but with the intention that all be served and enriched, that all be cherished and upheld?"

Our ability to accept what comes to us, even in the difficult or painful circumstances of our lives, enables us to learn about and experience the true power of love.

This work is the greatest and most demanding challenge that any of us are asked to undertake. The more of life we can accept, the more of love we are able to give and receive.

PART TWO

TOWARD WHOLENESS

Embracing Our Emotions and Desires

Deeper Yearnings

*M*any of our desires mask a deeper yearning. If we crave to own beautiful things, for example, this may well reflect the desire to know our own beauty and live in its grace. If we compulsively seek power over others, our underlying urge may be a longing to overcome our feelings of helplessness and create a sense of inner security. If we seek fame, we may in fact be seeking to transcend the fear of our own insignificance and to create a feeling of value and self-worth.

When we have an inclination toward self-pity, and can be found complaining about our lives, a core of truth usually underlies our behavior. Perhaps a pain that we carry is trying to draw our attention so that it may be acknowledged and finally healed. The complaining is our wounded attempt to call out for help. What is needed may be a willingness to seek out and work with the pain that is hidden underneath the self-pity.

The human spirit can be twisted and compressed, but the instinct toward wholeness is never destroyed. However distorted it may become, we can never completely lose the urge to say yes to life. Underpinning all our efforts, even those that seem the most fixated and compulsive, is the yearning to love and be loved.

Hidden Feelings

When many of us were young, we received the message that it wasn't safe to feel all of our feelings. As we learned to stifle our emotions, especially the "negative" ones, we also began to repress our very sense of aliveness, the aliveness that fuels our urge and capacity to feel and grow. We became afraid of our own feelings, unaware that they could become a source of knowledge, energy, and power.

Only through allowing deeply buried emotions to come to the surface can we become free from their inner pressure. Discovering the feelings that have been hidden away releases enormous energy into our lives. Even the wounds we have suffered can become a rich source of understanding, wisdom, and connection. As we open to feeling the reality of our inner lives, we find trees not only blossoming but also bearing fruit in the very spots where our old pains have been put to rest.

Learning From Our Reactions

Whenever we judge another person in a negative way, this judgment is a mirror that reflects what needs healing within ourselves. We accuse others of our own vices. We blame them for the very things for which we ourselves feel guilty. Even though their actions may be unconscious or abusive, the way in which we react says more about us than it does about them. Our challenge is to break the chain of our own self-judgment.

Whenever there is a misunderstanding, one part of us may react with aversion and defensiveness, while another part seeks to bring peace and understanding to the situation. This misunderstanding offers us a moment of choice. For it is in this moment, in the gap just before we react, that we have the power to choose consciously how we will respond. At first, the gap is fleeting and almost imperceptible. It may feel as if there is no choice at all, only an instantaneous, impulsive reaction. But as our understanding and clarity grow, the gap widens, until finally we have all the time we need to reflect quietly upon and choose those actions that are most closely aligned with our true desires.

The freedom not to react is as central to a conscious life as is the ability to respond. When a passionate and feeling heart learns the art of discernment, the door to wisdom and grace is opened.

Self-Work

*E*verything we do is a balancing and rebalancing, just as when we walk we must place one foot ahead and then lift the other. We would go nowhere if we always stood firmly balanced on both feet. At any given moment, it might appear that one of our two feet remains behind, seeming as if it hasn't yet caught up with the rest of us. Yet it is with this very foot that we push off to go forward.

Just so, when there is an area in our life that does not seem to be as far along as the rest of us, it is our push-off point, the very point by which we move forward toward a more fully integrated self.

It is tempting to view those parts of ourselves that trail behind as flaws. But they have been given to us for a very specific purpose. If we did not have them to work with, how could we learn to create what our hearts seek to fashion? They give us character and dimension, depth, contour, and interest. Our work is not to do away with problems, but to use them wisely.

Guilt and Remorse

*A*n important distinction exists between remorse, which can be a healthy and useful response when we have caused another pain, and guilt, which amounts to blaming and chastising ourselves.

Guilt is the belief that we are essentially bad, and therefore must be punished — punished for being ourselves, and then punished for punishing ourselves. At one moment, guilt moans, "I've failed! It's my fault." And the next moment, it points a finger and cries, "No, it wasn't my fault; someone else must be to blame." Guilt breeds both self-pity and blame.

Remorse is another matter. It arises in our true conscience, and comes not to demean us in any way, but to bring forth the highest in us. In its clearest form, remorse is actually a prayer of gratitude. We are saying, "Thank you for letting me see my ignorance. I am saddened by my past unconsciousness, and yet I am aware that I didn't know better, and could not see what I was doing. Now I am grateful for this opportunity to see more clearly how I can live the kind of life I so deeply want."

When we can say, "I have made a mistake, and I have learned from it and I will be more conscious in the future," we no longer have to justify our errors, or defend ourselves in any way. We have learned to live graciously with our own foolishness.

Acceptance

*T*he dance of life has many moods. The human heart is not always meant to be gay, any more than sunlight is always meant to be bright. There are nights; there is a time for silence, and a time for grief. There are moments of disillusionment and mourning. In the music of life, there are passages whose beauty is revealed only when played in the key of loss.

It is in acceptance that the mind and heart become free. Just as autumn yields to the coming of winter, so does winter receive the awakening of spring.

PART THREE

LIVING A CONSCIOUS LIFE

The Rhythms of Growth

Adversity

*A*dversity is not sent to harm us, but to help us develop our strength and resourcefulness. When we find ourselves entering an abyss, and having to face our own insecurities and fears, willingly or unwillingly, we are being offered an opportunity to awaken powers that have long lain dormant within us, powers that have been waiting for these particular conditions to arise so that our hidden capacities can be brought into being.

Life is not given to us because it will be easy. It is given to us because we are capable of it. Each sorrow that we have had to encounter testifies to the tremendous courage it takes to live a human life fully.

Our wounds speak not of our weakness, but of our bravery.

Discontent

*D*iscontent only arises in us when there is something in our lives that needs room to grow and expand. Just as a snake must struggle to release itself from an old skin that has grown too small, so must we periodically free ourselves from old ways that once served us, but that now hold us captive.

We are bound to encounter situations that require us to struggle to become more aware. We are bound to meet obstacles that make our lives difficult and demanding. These experiences invite us to affirm that the freedom of becoming more fully ourselves is worth the effort of confronting the difficulties, and worth all the struggle it may take to become more fully alive.

❧

Not Knowing

When we demand too much certainty in life, and ask for too many guarantees, we frustrate ourselves and tie up an immense amount of our energy.

When, however, we are able to live without certainty, comfortable with the paradoxes of life, answers have a way of arriving in their own time. In order to be at ease with the rhythms of existence, we need a sense of curiosity and wonder. We need to be able to face the insecurities of life with an eternal question in our heart, rather than a constant demand for immediate answers.

Not knowing is as necessary to the learning process as an empty mouth is to feeding.

Patience

*O*ur minds have two wonderful aspects. One part probes, doubts, and questions the meaning of existence. It seeks to build concepts and ideas that will satisfy its curiosity and need for precision. The other aspect listens to, and receives from, every impression that it is given, and then intuits a pattern, an overall view.

The rational mind functions in the universe of doing, and so must work logically on a problem. But the intuitive mind belongs within the unfathomable world of Being, and cannot do anything to hasten the moment of insight except to watch, wait, and listen.

In times of confusion, when our logical minds have exhausted themselves, it is essential that we cultivate patience. For we are always gathering things together in the depths of ourselves that will, at the right moment, gel into clarity and understanding.

Observation

*T*here seem to be two schools of thought on which attitude is best to assume when facing a difficult circumstance in life. One says to feel all our emotions fully. The other says to be dispassionate and unattached to all that life brings.

But we can no more try to be dispassionate when we are filled with deep emotion than we can be passionate when we feel emotionally void. We feel what we feel; we respond the way we respond. We may try to suppress an emotional response or sidestep it, but it will come again until we are able to understand the meaning it has for our life.

Each one of us resonates with life in a totally unique way. Some of us vibrate deeply from the heart, and we are given to passionate emotional responses. Others of us are moved more powerfully by the mind, and we tend to respond more thoughtfully. But whatever type of personality we have, it is valuable to cultivate for ourselves a quality of observation, an ability to witness and become aware of our own reactions, to learn from them, accept them, and ultimately to free ourselves from their unconscious hold upon us.

It is not a question of whether one response is right and another is wrong; it is a question of watching to see whether our responses bear the fruit we would wish.

Different Paths

One of the hardest things we are asked to do is to recognize that no one else's path is any more or any less sacred than our own.

Some paths are certainly far easier than others. Some are comparatively clean and direct, illumined by fine inner qualities and clearly guided by spirit. Other paths are more harsh and tense, burdened by self-destructive habits and shadowed by seemingly needless pain.

For some of us, life has many roses. We seem naturally and effortlessly to rise to the challenges we are offered. For others, life has many thorns. Despite our best efforts, we find ourselves repeatedly mired in patterns of darkness and confusion. Yet who is to say which of us is learning more, growing more deeply, or contributing more lastingly to the heart of all that is?

Being open and reverent to another's path doesn't mean colluding with that person in patterns to which we are opposed. It means honoring the heart of those with whom we differ. We don't have to understand or agree with other people's decisions in order to respect and uphold their worthiness.

PART FOUR

OUR FEARS AS FUEL

Moving Toward Faith and Joy

Transforming Fear

We each have our own personal black holes into which we sometimes fall, and through which we partake of the fear that has dominated the human psyche for aeons. Many of us are now feeling an urge, even a sense of responsibility, to see this fear transformed. We are learning that this fear can only be transformed within the family, the community, and the world if it is also being transformed within ourselves — and if we are doing the necessary personal work, so that one day we can finally say that we have learned to live harmoniously with one another and to be enriched by our differences rather than threatened by them.

Breaking Free From Fear

When we look back at the times when we have been afraid, and recall what it was we feared, we can often see just how exaggerated and untrue were the images produced by our fears.

Fearful thoughts try to trick us into believing they are real, but they have no power other than the power that we give to them.

We are wealthy not by the measure of our possessions, but according to what does not possess us. The freedom not to be bothered by fearful thoughts is not the freedom from fearful thoughts. It is the freedom to see that they are merely thoughts. As we become more able to discern what fear actually is and what it is not, we begin the process of breaking its hypnotic trance.

Fear of God

*T*he belief in the possibility of a punishing judgment after death has been instilled and reinforced in us down through history by religions and belief systems that have been based in fear. But now increasing numbers of us are realizing that such beliefs do not bring out the best in us. They rob us of our ability to hear directly the promptings of our own heart.

It is only the human mind, when it is beset by fear and guilt, that judges and punishes, and then foolishly attributes this smallness to the source of the stars.

Risk and Faith

There is a special exhilaration that comes with deliberately facing our fears, with taking risks on behalf of our growth. Just as children may love the experience of a roller coaster, even though it frightens them, we may find it thrilling to choose consciously to encounter the situations that tend to trigger our fears. When we have an inner confidence that we can find a way of coping with whatever comes our way, then we become able to take chances, and thus invite into our lives a renewed sense of aliveness and excitement. Our fears no longer paralyze us, but become instead the very backdrop against which we find out how courageous we actually are.

Faith is not a matter of trusting that events will always occur to our liking, but of trusting that, whatever happens, our inner resources will be equal to the moment.

PART FIVE

THE ALCHEMY OF ANGER

Living Our Passion

Anger

*A*nger is an intense and primal expression of the life force, a burning flame that cannot be ignored. It is the psyche's alarm system, demanding that attention be given to a limit or boundary of ours that is being invaded, to a pain or need that is being denied, or to an area of our being that has become unhealthy.

The function of anger is similar to the function of a fever. It helps to burn out unwanted, inharmonious elements. Its purpose is to restore balance and well-being.

If the symptoms of a fever are suppressed and ignored, then the illness will remain unchecked. So it is with anger. It is useful to listen for the message it brings and then to use it for growth and wellness.

We need to remember that the anger we feel toward someone else is not an accurate evaluation or judgment of who that person actually is. It is merely our own feelings communicating with us, telling us more about ourselves than about the other person. It is the beginning of greater clarity and discrimination, so that we can live our passion with integrity, develop our inner power, and become capable of acting assertively, rather than aggressively, on behalf of what we cherish.

Anger With an Open Heart

*T*here should really be two different words: one for "anger-with-the-heart-closed," and one for "anger-with-the-heart-open."

Most anger in our society is "anger-with-the-heart-closed." Many of us are in the habit of automatically using our anger vindictively to protect ourselves or to impose our will upon others. We may believe ourselves totally justified in demeaning others' self-esteem. We may believe that we do this for "their own good." We may even believe that the will we are trying to impose is God's will. From such unconsciousness have come generations of abuse. From such self-righteousness have come millennia of "holy" wars.

"Anger-with-the-heart-closed" is destructive. But there are times when our anger can be a gift to the other person, when it is not simply our own ego twisting in a knot, and trying to use the other person to undo the strain. Though we may feel great heat and urgency, there need be nothing mean in the way we express ourselves. For when there is no desire to wound or punish or blame, we become able to speak with great clarity and power. We may roar like a lion, but it is a healing roar. We may be challenging, but we are infinitely fair. We may be outraged, but we are respectful. This is "anger-with-the-heart-open," and it has a beauty, a passion, and a clarity that is unmistakable.

48

Saying No

*N*o can be a beautiful word, every bit as beautiful as *yes*. Whenever we deny our need to say no, our self-respect diminishes.

It is not only our right at certain times to say no; it is our deepest responsibility. For it is a gift to ourselves when we say no to those old habits that dissipate our energy, no to what robs us of our joy, no to what distracts us from our purpose. And, it is a gift to others to say no when their expectations do not ring true for us, for in so doing we free them to discover more fully the truth of their own path. Saying no can be liberating when it expresses our commitment to take a stand for what we truly need.

If we find ourselves being inauthentically "nice," saying yes when we mean no, this can be our opportunity to bring an unwanted fear in ourselves to the light. Through such self-honesty, we can reclaim our source of personal power, inner joy, and self-esteem.

Handling Others' Anger

*I*f we become anxious and defensive when someone is angry with us, might it be that the anger is not the real source of our discomfort? Is it possible that the anger has brought to the surface our own self-judgment and doubt?

If someone were angry with us for having three heads, we wouldn't feel guilty or worry about whether it was actually true or not. We wouldn't feel that it was impossible to be happy until we had proven to that person that actually we have only one head. But if someone's anger toward us touches a raw nerve, then we are being shown where our loving attention is needed.

When we are able to accept our shortcomings without any self-recrimination, then we are released from the curse of always trying to appear perfect. When we have come to peace with our imperfections, we can accept in our own nature both the light and its shadow.

PART SIX

THE ESSENCE OF HEALING

Awakening True Compassion

The Instinct Toward Health

*I*f our life energy is bottled up or blocked, it loses its momentum. We become unmotivated, exhausted, and bored, and eventually we may become ill. But when we are excited by our continual participation in life, when we are giving ourselves to a purpose and a work that we love, when our lives are attuned to our inner natures, then our inherent healing powers are activated. We not only become less susceptible to disease, but our instincts become increasingly clear, reliable, and healthy.

Illness

*T*here is a tendency in some of us, if we become ill, to feel guilty, as if our discomfort were a sign that we have failed, or that we are being punished for wrong thinking or wrong action. We sometimes act as if the degree of our health were a statement of our value, or of our level of consciousness.

But illness is not a chastisement or a punishment. It is the body's way of seeking equilibrium, of restoring true health, of bringing mind, body, and spirit into harmony. Though it is a journey that can be discouraging and painful, it can also be rich with possibilities for inner work and growth. It enables us to disengage our feelings of self-worth from our outer performance, and to reconnect with something more eternal.

If an illness is the consequence of living habits that are disrespectful to our bodies or to our spirits, then we have an opportunity to heed the message and make the changes called for, bringing our life into greater alignment with nature's laws. This is a time to reevaluate our priorities and rededicate ourselves to what we truly cherish. It is a time when the remembrance of death looms near, and so it is a time to remember and cultivate great appreciation and friendliness toward life. Even our afflictions can become initiations into a closer relationship with our essential self.

Accepting Others' Pain

Our ability to feel compassion is greatly enhanced if we are able to be in the presence of pain, our own or another's, and yet still retain our balance and keep our heart open and calm. Many of us want to keep the ones we love happy, and may find it difficult to see them in pain. We want them to be pleased with us, to be healthy and well, and, if they are not, we may judge ourselves harshly, fearing that we have failed.

And yet, once we make peace with pain, and accept it as an essential and at times unavoidable part of life, we can embrace those we love even when they suffer. All pain, at some level, can be a gift. Though we might wish to spare the ones we love from pain, we can realize that, if we would not steal from them their joy, it would be senseless to wish to rob them of their sorrow.

Pity and Compassion

*T*here is an essential difference between pity and compassion.

Pity believes that the one pitied is incapable of choosing wisely, and so seeks to instruct and correct. Pity discounts the inner wisdom of the other. Even when it thinks itself kind, pity sees the other as inferior, and so can actually act as a subtle form of domination.

True compassion, on the other hand, is given freely, with no hidden motive, no desire of changing another. It is motivated by a profound respect for the capability, intelligence, and strength at the core of each and every person. It acknowledges the validity of all paths to awakening, and the inherent ability of every soul to learn from all experiences. The person with compassion has no need to be seen as being the bringer of healing.

Pity believes in, and gives power to, the temporary appearances and circumstances of life. Compassion never forgets the immutable Being that exists beyond those appearances.

PART SEVEN

LONELINESS AND ALONENESS

Becoming a Light Unto Oneself

Loneliness

*L*oneliness is the soul's longing for itself. It is the soul's urge to be one with its own silence, to be full with its own aliveness, not to go searching over mountains for another to fill its cup, but to drink from its own well. It is the longing to be complete, as the hills are complete, as wind and light and stone are complete.

There are times in every human journey when we must seemingly walk alone, for the rite of passage that is called loneliness has a purpose. It throws us upon our own inner resources, so that we can discover our own rhythms and integrity.

It is an opportunity to know ourselves more fully, to become more whole, and to become more capable of true friendship and love.

Being Single

*I*n today's world, many of us are living without the experience of a supportive community. Many of us are living without the security of knowing that we belong, without the comfort of being able to reach out at any time in order to receive assistance and love, without the reassurance of feeling ourselves to be an essential part of communal life. Yet we are social beings who need intimacy, nurturing, and a sense of connection.

Those of us who are not sharing our lives with a partner, or who find ourselves in the difficult situation of being a single parent, often feel painfully alone. Though the feeling of rootlessness and the loss of communion can be excruciating, many of us are being challenged to meet this pain and to use it in order to grow in extraordinary new ways.

Being single is not a time to search desperately for a partner or a family. It is an opportunity to remember and reconnect with the strength of our own intrinsic wholeness. For many of us, it is a time to uncover and work with our feelings of self-pity, abandonment, and loneliness, and to heal that part of ourselves that does not believe itself to be worthy of support. It is a time for showing compassion toward ourselves, for finding new ways of ministering to our own needs.

Love Lost

We would do well to have a special place for the heartsick, for those who are mourning because they have turned a corner and can never return, for those who have lost a dream that once flowed with possibility, for those whose quest for love has grown empty and cold.

When we have risked loving with our whole heart, and have later come to feel bereft, it is tempting to blame ourselves for being so vulnerable, or to blame the other for having betrayed us. It takes great courage to remain open to giving and receiving love when the gift comes so interwoven with sorrow.

The pain of a love that has been unrequited or even exploited need not be in vain. If, in our heart and mind, we are able to question openly and inquire, even as we mourn, we will be able to use our grief for self-realization rather than self-pity. And, as we live through and complete our sorrow, learning all we can from each experience as we go along, we will discover in ourselves the wisdom to discern when we are ready to love and trust once more.

The Inner Calling

*J*ust as the salmon pursues its course upstream, as if drawn by an irresistible magnet toward its destiny, so does each human being follow an inner calling. This inner calling speaks to us through our feelings, our intuitions, and our deepest urges. A young child with a destiny to be a musician often delights in music and feels drawn to play an instrument.

Those experiences that cause us to feel most alive and most conscious are the very experiences that, when we listen to them, will lead us toward our destiny. We are being pulled forward by our own potential.

PART EIGHT

THE GREAT HARMONY

Balancing Masculine and Feminine Energies

Sun and Moon

*F*or centuries, the sun has been taken to symbolize the masculine aspect of creation; the moon, the feminine. The fact that these heavenly bodies appear to be precisely the same size to the human eye is a reminder of the great symmetry at the core of life.

The Great Spirit lives both in darkness and in light, and there is power in each realm. The power of the day is the power of doing. It finds expression in our abilities to think and to act. The power of the night is the power of being. It lives in our abilities to sense, to feel, and to intuit.

Our culture has become so achievement oriented and outer directed that we may not realize, when our daytime consciousness becomes confused trying to understand something, that it may be a time to rest, a time to trust the darkness, the night, the quiet, and the feminine.

When our culture has achieved genuine equality for men and women, when each of us as an individual is able to give equal voice to the masculine and the feminine aspects of our own being, then the level of intelligence in our world will rise dramatically.

Male and Female

*T*he basic relationship between the two halves of humanity, between the masculine and feminine, has over the centuries become shadowed by distrust, competition, withholding, and domination. Our relationships often reflect our society's unresolved tensions, unmet expectations, and heartbreaking disappointments.

There are many of us now who want to be finished with this grief. We are asking how the feminine and masculine can positively and authentically work together to support each other, not only within the dynamic of a couple, but in the greater world, and in the consciousness of ourselves as individuals. How can we transform the conditioning that has rendered us suspicious, afraid of being exploited, and thus distant from our own power, passion, and wholeness?

The male dimension of our culture's psyche will never be at peace until it recovers its reverence for the feminine. Yet in order for us to respect, treasure, and yield to the female instinctive wisdom, we must see what we have been conditioned to project onto the feminine energy.

In many of us, the masculine dimension of ourselves is learning to say to the feminine, "In you I see the forces

I have feared, the chaos I have tried to control, the Earth-mother I have been taught to exploit. I have been conditioned to deny you, to see in you the prospect of emotions running out of control. I have thought it necessary to dominate and repress you so that life might feel more ordered and contained. I have often treated you as inferior and have disdained your intelligence because it was different from my own. I have felt important by holding you as unimportant, and I have felt powerful by demeaning you.

"But now a shift is taking place. I am beginning to realize that I am here to support you that you may live the full power of your spontaneous nature. I am learning to listen to your vision and to help it become a reality. I am learning to honor your rhythms and healing urges, knowing it is safe for you to settle into the depths of yourself, to purge, renew, and express that which has reached its time. I want to call you forth, to embrace you, and rejoice in your power. I want to learn and grow with you, to take pleasure in our differences, and to be drawn to life by your mystery."

As the dominant/submissive model of relationship gives way to a partnership model, the feminine aspect of our being is realizing just how devalued, depreciated, and humiliated she has been. As she begins to feel worthy of respect, she may feel not only sadness for what has been lost, but anger at the patriarchal and patronizing paradigm that has caused so much separation and pain. She grows in the power to arise and object whenever life is not respected.

Whether manifesting through a man or a woman, the feminine spirit reminds us that love is wiser than fear, and that all are worthy of compassion. She rises up against social systems that are ruled by violence or the threat of loss, and replaces hierarchic and authoritarian family systems and social structures with ones based in trust. She upholds that genuine power is not the ability to dominate or control, but the capacity to respond, to support, care for, and nurture all of life.

As the feminine dimension of our consciousness gathers strength, we begin to see what over the years has been projected onto the male. The feminine might say, "I have been conditioned to see you as a tyrant who will not be countered or questioned, and I have obeyed you out of fear. Expecting you to be given the credit for everything, and for my support to go unnoticed, I have depreciated myself and have ignored my own contribution.

"Assuming your wisdom to be more rational, I have distrusted and subdued the flame of my own creative intelligence, and I have backed away from my own power. I have experienced your needs as valid, important, and essential, but I have negated my own. In this, I have not been a true partner to you, for I have believed that you wanted me to diminish myself, rather than to express my integrity and develop my strength.

"I have seen how the placing of one half of humanity over the other has poisoned all human relations, and I do not wish to exchange places with you and come to hold myself above you. Together, as partners, we must recognize that we are a part of each other's wholeness.

"I see how you have been hurt by your separation from me. I see how you have been trained to hold yourself aloof, to deny your weakness, and I can see the pain that this has caused you. I am here to see you grow strong and unafraid of your emotions, and to help you know that the heart is as much a teacher as the mind. I hold you in love as you return to me, and I watch over you as you remember to cherish all that gives life."

Together, they might say: "We are a union. And within that union can be seen the workings of the sacred mystery. We bring each other laughter and warmth, challenge and learning. We can touch each other's wounds with healing, respect each other's mystery, and call forth from each other a life that has meaning. Together, we can act on behalf of what we treasure. Without each other, we are incomplete, but with each other we can fulfill our destinies and bring a better world into being."

Menstruation

*T*he female menstrual cycle has been called a curse. But it can be a gift to those women who take the time to appreciate the mystery of this very special phase of the moon. The monthly release is not merely a natural physical cleansing; it is also a time nature has provided for a profound renewal of a woman's inward life. Her sensitivities are heightened, and her moods more richly colored. This can be a time of great inner depth and learning.

There can be conflict, however, if a woman tries to engage too much with the world. There is a need for her to allow her energy to move inward and down, to allow her spirit to restore and reconnect with inner resources.

A woman may become aware, during this time, of aspects in her life that call for healing. She may realize that things she has been doing, choices that she has been making, or people with whom she has been interacting are no longer appropriate for her. These awarenesses are being brought to her attention so that she can align her life more fully with her heart.

The disintegration that occurs as old forms break down, allowing the new to emerge, can be confusing. Yet during this phase, a woman is under the protection of the moon, the Mother, the feminine. This is a time to receive the gifts of her magic and mystery. It is a time to listen, to intuit, to let go of what has been and to be receptive to what is yet to be.

PART NINE

THE TREE OF LIFE

Love, Sexuality, and Intimacy

Sex and Love

*T*here is a dynamic relationship between sexual energy and love. They interrelate deeply; they work together to bind creation into a wonderfully cohesive whole.

Love is like the tree of life, with its trunk, roots, branches, leaves, and fruit. Sexual energy is like the sap moving within this tree. It is the current that transports nourishment and vitality to every cell of the whole.

Sexual energy is not merely the urge toward reproduction. This is but one small expression of its purpose. For just as love is an expression of the ultimate oneness of all life, the sexual force is the living, breathing energy of polarity within that oneness.

It is the energy of attraction and repulsion. It is what draws together and propels apart, what unites and separates. It is a wave that ebbs and flows, that waxes and wanes, that builds and declines, creates and destroys.

The urge toward consummation is where sexual energy is most obviously identified, but it is this same energy that builds temples, plants gardens, writes books, and adventures into the unknown. It is this same energy that invents, aspires, inquires, and evokes.

And it is this same energy, when blocked, that leads to war and destruction, and then once more strives to rebuild.

Sexual energy is the call of the future and the drive toward expansion. It is the ever-present insistence of life that everything continually evolve.

All this action and movement, this pulsating life force, this ongoing transformation, is the flow of sap moving within the eternal tree of life, which is love.

Sexuality

*I*n our culture, after hundreds of years of sexual denial, the pendulum has swung the other way. Now our society has a preoccupation with sexuality. There is hardly a place where its mark cannot be found. All this makes it difficult to feel the deeply personal, intimate, and holy function that sexual energy can play in our lives.

Despite the degree to which sexuality permeates the culture, the collective guilt of history can still be felt. We have been socialized to be suspicious of pleasure, to live removed from our bodies, and to maintain a tight rein over our feelings. In a culture riddled with guilt, sexual confusion, and body shame, the sexual force has often been misused. Yet when entered with joy, tenderness, and respect, it becomes not only a source of great vitality, but a guide to the ways of the heart.

We are entrusted with our sexual appetite, power, and capacity for feeling not so that we will be driven by it, but so that we may be nourished and upheld, strengthened and moved. The flow of sexual excitement in the body is, in and of itself, a healing gift. There need be nothing about our sexual experience that removes us from the sacred. In fact, sexual union can be the ritual expression that unites body and spirit in a divine dance of Creation.

Sexual Conflicts Between Partners

*B*ecause we are evolving beings, our need or lack of need for sexual expression will flux and change. It may sometimes feel impossible for two people to remain harmonious in a mutual level of desire for any prolonged length of time. There is tremendous understanding available if we are able to listen deeply whenever a lack of harmony arises between us. We are gift bearers, bringing messages to ourselves and to one another through our sexual sharing. The ability to remain still enough to hear these messages requires tremendous discipline—the discipline of not complaining, of not blaming, of not fearing or doubting or judging. It is, in fact, the ultimate discipline of unconditional love and curiosity.

There are many reasons why two people are drawn sexually to one another. There is the need to be reassured, to reassure the other, to forget separateness, to be safe, to feel alive and vibrant, to be united, to feel in communion with, to ward off loneliness, to feel valued, to be momentarily complete, to do our duty, to transcend the daily boredom, to touch the mysterious, to awaken the life force, to be consumed by a power greater than the mind, to heal misunderstandings, to claim our territory, to reinstate our affectionate hold, to give what we believe the other wants, to keep peace, to express tenderness, and on and on and on. All of the reasons are valid; all of them are part of a deep urge toward wholeness and love.

But each different reason carries with it a different energy field. Some of these fields are mutually compatible, and some are not. If, for example, we are longing to be reassured that we are loved and valued, and our partner is giving what he or she considers to be a duty, neither of us will be satisfied.

During times of disconnectedness, if we can intimately and with deep trust venture together into our most vulnerable honesties, we will begin to discover there the understanding that can eventually lead to healing.

We have been given few attributes as potent, volatile, and complex as our sexuality. For our sexuality often becomes a focal point where unacknowledged fears, hopes, expectations, and griefs rise to the surface.

It takes courage to go beyond our fear and actually acknowledge what is buried within us, but, when we do, we open the way for communion, joy, and profound discovery.

The more we can share about ourselves with our beloved, the more sexual harmony we will enjoy, and the greater will be our ability to discover and heal all the fears and misconceptions that keep us from our true capacity for intimacy, pleasure, and fulfillment.

Intimacy and Humility

We have been socialized in this culture to believe in a romantic fantasy in which two people meet, fall in love, live happily ever after, and never need anyone else.

This, we all eventually discover, is merely a fairy tale, and seeking it distracts us from the possibility of a more fulfilling voyage of discovery, a voyage that can lead us deeper into ourselves and into each other.

Inevitably, we bring not only our love to a relationship, but also our wounds and confusion. As the relationship begins to mature, we become a bit more willing to let go of the image that we believed we needed to maintain in order to love or to be loved. We become willing to risk showing more of ourselves, more of those places where we believe we are flawed.

Healing relationships give us the courage to face ourselves, to see those attitudes and behaviors that are not in keeping with our essential being. They show us the ways in which we distance ourselves from others, and enable us to see how we defend those habits and beliefs that compromise our well-being and the well-being of our relationships. As we acknowledge and share these patterns, they can become undone. Conflict, guilt, sorrow, and all the other fearful emotions can lead us to the place where the wounded child waits in hiding, so that what has been hurt can be brought to health.

When our heart's desire is to heal ourselves and each other, then every single moment can become an invitation to move toward love. When we open to ourselves and to our beloved with honor and total acceptance, something miraculous happens. In the full mingling of our spirits we are renewed, strengthened, and delivered to our highest possibilities. Our love has become a bridge not only to ourselves and to each other, but to life itself.

Criticism and Intimacy

*T*here are times in every intimate relationship when we wish to express to the other person that he or she is doing something that we feel is not in alignment with his or her spirit.

This is a delicate moment. For when we share any kind of criticism, the attitude we hold toward the other and the manner in which we speak are an essential part of the message we convey. The communication becomes difficult to receive if we are relating out of a sense of separation or condescension, if we are bitter, judgmental, or angry or if we are needing the other person to change. There is a much greater possibility that our communication will be heard and received when we are embracing the other as essentially well and whole, and when we speak with acceptance and respect for who he or she already is.

We have all at times used our intimate relationships as a place to vent our frustrations. A healing relationship, however, calls for impeccable responsibility and infinite fairness and respect. For only then can enough trust develop so that trembling hearts can open deeply to each other and risk being known.

PART TEN

THE CYCLES OF LIFE

Honoring Our Different Roles

Parents

When we arrived on this planet, we found ourselves plunged into a state of complete vulnerability. We looked to our parents with the natural expectation that they would supply all the love, support, and consciousness from which we had become so suddenly separated.

We looked to our parents to be perfect for us. We did not know that the human beings into whose care we had taken birth had their own troubles. There is no way we could have known that they were fallible, that they were also worried by feelings of loneliness, anger, sadness, and fear. No matter how much they loved and welcomed us, they were in many ways still children themselves, longing to be protected and healed from their own pain, insecurity, and disappointment.

Every being is wounded as he or she takes on a human destiny. And if our parents were not able to give to us their respect and love, we can be assured that it was their wounding that caused them to treat us thus, and not their essential self.

The fear and guilt we received from our parents did not originate in them. They in turn received many of their anxieties from their parents, and so on back through the lineage of human suffering.

Once our parents were like gods to us. But for each of us there comes a time when we learn to see them for the human beings that they are. We are asked to acknowledge that even if they were cruel they did not in truth mean us harm, but were only ignorantly acting out the ancient pain of a humanity that has barely begun to live its potential for love.

The more fully we allow ourselves the wisdom and discernment to appreciate our parents exactly as they are, the greater will be our joy and pride in ourselves, the more successful will be all of our relationships, and the richer will be our contribution to the child that dwells within each person we meet.

Adolescents and Parents

*I*n our culture today, there are few rites of passage that actually acknowledge and celebrate a young person's crossing over into adulthood. Boys are not welcomed openly by older men. Girls are not consciously invited to be a part of the women's world. Thus, what frequently happens is that our youngsters must secretly try to discover their own place in adult society, and must somewhat randomly attempt to claim their own manhood or womanhood. Consequently, for most, puberty is fraught with confusion and anxiety.

Today's young people are being bombarded through the media with sexual messages that stimulate and entice. And yet, at the same time, they are being cautioned and warned that their emerging sexuality can be dangerous. Under the circumstances, is it any wonder that they find it difficult to discern and understand their own feelings? Now, more than ever, teenagers need to be encouraged to share their sexual fears and questions in an open way. And yet, because so few of their parents or teachers are comfortable with their own sexuality, intimate and loving communication is often unavailable to them.

Puberty is a crucial turning point in the process of individuation. As young people become biologically capable of procreating their own families, the urge develops to expand beyond the family unit they have known in order to form their relationship with the larger community. Suddenly, there is a sense of needing to venture forth, to have a say in the direction in which the world is going, and yet at the very same time there is often a fear of presuming to do so.

This is not a time to expect consistency from young people. At one moment, they will behave with precocious maturity and independence, but then in the next moment they will express a need for us to watch over them as though they were much younger. Part adult and part child, they may feel literally torn between their past and their future. They are often suspended precariously between two different realities, and the bridge across which they must pass is frequently beset by storms and swayed by heavy winds.

As parents, it is our task and privilege to be a safety net for them at these times. If we are able to understand and encourage rather than criticize, to guide rather than correct, then we can become a source of companionship and support as they journey through all the shifting moods of adolescence.

In cultures that ritualize the initiation of youth into adulthood, young people are given direct permission by their elders to claim their new status in the community. They are respected as having graduated into the next phase of human development.

But in those cultures where there are no such initiations, it is given to individual parents to guide their children through this transition. The greatest gifts we can give them during this powerful time in their lives are our respect, our openness, our heartfelt communication, and our loving acceptance. In this way, they can know that we honor them deeply as they pass through what nature has decreed to be the most dramatic physical transition in a person's life, other than birth and death.

Guides on the Journey

*T*here will always be different types of guides. There are those who are humble and grateful simply to be of use. They may have personal magnetism and power, but they never exert any kind of domination over anyone. Instead, they take sincere delight in all kinds of people, knowing that no one person is more or less important than another.

And there are also those teachers whose motivation is tainted with self-aggrandizement, who are entranced by power and status. Their teachings often increase fear and self-judgment, and cause us to feel dependent on them.

It is inevitable that our judgment will at times be faulty, that we may consider someone to be more trustworthy than he or she later turns out to be. And though we may feel betrayed, we are learning something that we could not learn in any other way. We have been granted the experience of disillusionment so that our power of discrimination may grow ever more keen in its ability to recognize truth.

The "false" guides we have known have served us by their very unconsciousness. They have been like a vaccine, causing us to become immune to the lure of something that would harm us.

There is nothing like intimacy with the "false" to show us the difference between that and what is true.

Abortion

*T*hose who are fanatically opposed to one another on the issue of abortion have something very similar and beautiful in common.

People who are ardently opposed to abortion are often responding to a deep yearning of the human spirit to remember that every baby is precious and should be wanted, that every soul who comes to Earth should be greeted with yes and not with no, that every fragile embryo should be respected and cherished. They sense that life is holy, and that every individual who undertakes the human journey deserves to be welcomed with open arms.

On the other side are those who passionately believe that a woman should have the right to determine her own destiny. These people are not insensitive to the call of life. Their experience tells them that requiring a woman to have a child she does not want will not provide that child with the welcome yes she or he so richly deserves. They feel a woman who truly doesn't want to be a mother would not be able to give the safety, the kindness, and the nurturance that every child should have.

At heart, many of the people on both sides want the same thing—to support and affirm life. Whenever we hold a decidedly different point of view from someone else, and we believe in it passionately and deeply, it is especially important to honor the humanity of those who do not share our same vision.

While at the surface it may seem to be a simple matter of right or wrong, there is a deeper opportunity in this polarization. It is a matter of human beings learning to be sensitive to the laws and wisdom of love.

If you are considering an abortion, it can be a profound experience to speak honestly and openheartedly to the being that has been conceived. You can pour your heart out to him or her, knowing that you are heard by one who understands. Then there will arise in you a knowing born of your true connection and commitment to yourself and to this being. Then you can act responsibly, without shame or guilt, with your actions attuned to your inner wisdom.

Life cannot ultimately be created or destroyed. It cannot be threatened. Only the mind, in its attachments, feels threatened. Death is not the end; it is just a horizon past which the five senses cannot see. Physical bodies come and go. Thoughts and ideas arise and pass away. But essential spirit, though it is forever changing, is immutably and eternally present.

The Moment of Conception

What is telling at conception is not our superficial state of mind, not our momentary mood, but our central purpose and commitment in life. The soul preparing to take birth is not that concerned with the temporary attitude of the moment, but is drawn to and profoundly affected by the spiritual reality of the beings who will be his or her parents. There is a bonding that takes place on a spirit level, by which the soul to be the child and the souls to be the mother and father come together and agree to intertwine destinies.

The act of lovemaking is so much more than a casual encounter; it is a uniting with the powers of Creation. The potential newcomer does not hear the sighs of the physical realm. It hears the song in our hearts, and it is this melody that calls it to life.

PART ELEVEN

In the Hands of Spirit

Expressing Our Spiritual Essence

Reverence

Our identity in this lifetime is but a single breath in a far greater life. We are part of billions of years of evolution on this planet. The energy that is in us has lived in billions upon billions of lifetimes in different forms.

Yet we are still only a beginning.

When we look at the stars and marvel at their awesome beauty, if we are most lucky, we may touch the seed of a larger mystery. With this sense of the miraculous, innocence and humility can awaken, and a temple of wonder can be built in our hearts. The meaning of all the suffering we have endured along the way, and all the choices we have made, is placed into perspective when we experience ourselves as a link in a chain that stretches further back into history and forward into the future than imagination can travel. In the light of this vast unfolding, we can begin to discover within ourselves an extraordinary capacity for amazement and gratitude, a feeling of utter reverence for the opportunity of a human life.

The One Source

*T*here is only one sun for our planet, even though different languages have different names for it. So, too, despite the many different religions and beliefs in different cultures, there is one common Source feeding the soul of all humanity.

It matters not what name we assign to this universal Source. We can call it by a particular name, or by no name at all, and it will still continue to nourish, guide, and sustain us.

The well from which we draw living spirit may be of brick or stone, and it may be deep or shallow, but if the water that comes from it is clean and fresh, then here may we go to drink, so that our thirst may be quenched.

The various religions are not meant to separate us; they are but sparks of understanding, flickers of the universal flame through which we can illuminate our lives.

Different Ways

*I*f a particular way of life helps us to become more connected with what we feel to be holy, if it makes us feel freer to discover and express love and understanding, then we should follow it. Yet in so doing, we must remember that other people have other ways, and that we, too, may have other ways at other times.

Every human being, every bird that sings, every blade of grass, every sunrise, is charged with something of the Divine. Every belief system, every philosophy, every idea, and every thought offers yet another glimpse into the infinite possibility that is life.

It can be tremendously valuable to open ourselves to new ways of experiencing the Divine. The ultimate consciousness of love and truth is, after all, far beyond what our wildest imaginings could ever possibly conceive.

Access to Spirit

$\mathcal{E}$very religious tradition has a dream of the Garden of Eden, the paradise lost. Every religion speaks of the longing for fulfillment, Salvation, Nirvana, Samadhi, the Kingdom of Heaven, the longing to return to the Source, to go home.

The many separate religions are like the many spokes of a wheel; they all stem from the same inner hub, and the same intrinsic desire for oneness with life. We are here to live in the center, not to be ground with every turn of the wheel.

The founders of the great religions did not think, "I am creating a new religion." They simply lived the spirit as they experienced and understood it. As others began to worship them, however, a crystallized institution was made out of what had once been a flowering and an inspiration. It is these institutions that have created rigid rules for human behavior, seeking to control and contain the human heart, rather than helping the individual to trust and express his or her own personal connection with the Divine.

If we feel guilty for who we are and for what is natural to us, we lose trust in our own wisdom, and become vulnerable to the suggestions of those in power even if their suggestions go against our own true instincts. Those of us who respect the authority of our own hearts cannot be convinced to do anything that does not rest easily with our highest inner promptings.

Prayer

*P*rayer is a most personal and intimate act. It does not really matter if we have no definite idea whom we are addressing. It is a way of opening ourselves, of establishing a resonance with the Infinite, whatever we conceive it to be. No two people come to prayer in the same way. For some, prayer is like chatting with a friend. For some, it is an emotional, passionate encounter. For others, prayer is more ritualized, evoking a stillness and a sense of mystery. For some, it is more abstract and refined. But whatever way we approach the sacred, prayer, like love, is a way of communing with life.

If we only pray when we want something, then our sense of what prayer can be becomes limited and small. If we were to sing only when we wanted something, we would miss much of the richness available through song. We would never sing to express joy or triumph, sorrow or love. We would never know that the wonder of song is that it can ritualize and bring beauty to all states of mind and all moods of the heart. So it is with prayer. Whether or not we are conscious of it, we are praying all the time. Our deepest strivings and longings are our prayers, and they are fashioning our lives continuously. Whatever our temporary state of mind, there persists the ongoing communication of our fundamental urges. Prayer is the ancient and primal language of the self.

Prayer, Dependence, and Self-Responsibility

*A*lthough prayer may begin as a plea for rescue, it can mature into something much richer—a willingness to face ourselves and our lives, and to be assisted in the process by the guiding forces of the Universe.

When we pray for someone to come and protect us from life's challenges, we are expressing our need for a dependent relationship with something outside of ourselves. But when we pray for wisdom and strength to arise from within us to meet our challenges, then we are creating an opening through which life can bring us clarity, compassion, and the courage to live fully.

Placing our lives in the hands of Spirit need not be an evasion of personal responsibility. It can be an opening to vaster powers, powers that are ever within us, waiting to arise and draw us home.

PART TWELVE

The Awakened Heart

Following Our Urge Toward Service

Confronting the World's Pain

When confronting the suffering of our time, it is easy to become overwhelmed. In a world with nuclear bombs, toxic wastes, massive cruelty, racism, starvation, and child abuse, in a world where species are extinguished every hour, is it any wonder that we sometimes fall into despair?

We do not have to be finished dealing with our own problems before we can make a contribution to the world. In fact, it is often by reaching out to others that our own healing takes place. As we bring our lives into balance, we see that our own happiness is somehow inexplicably linked to the happiness of all beings.

This does not mean that those of us who seek to be of service must take too much responsibility upon ourselves. For when we do, we begin to feel drained and empty, we become righteous and intolerant, and we experience no joy. It is difficult at times to realize that we are not here to save anyone else, and that in fact sometimes the greatest gift we can give to others is the respect of trusting that they are in the hands of a greater intelligence.

We often forget that we are not the sole source of help on this planet. There are colossal forces at work in the Universe with powers of regeneration and healing that are beyond our comprehension. They are here, supporting our every effort to become whole and free.

Our Simple Role
in the Great Turning

*N*othing is more natural than the desire to contribute to others. Yet many of us judge ourselves for the amount of help we are able to offer, or compare our gifts or our achievements with those of others. We do not always see that whatever we do when our hearts are committed and full of compassion becomes woven into the very fabric of existence.

Sometimes we may say to ourselves, "I am not doing enough; I should do more. Look how much others are doing. . . ." Although we may be attempting to motivate ourselves to acts of concern for others, such self-belittlement only makes us feel ashamed.

Our urge toward service does not thrive in the soil of guilt; it grows more surely in an atmosphere of self-acceptance and authentic caring. This is the kind of caring that can accept our simple role in this great turning, and can act upon the desire to see the world a bit healthier, happier, saner, more ethical, and more beautiful in whatever way best suits our nature.

We help to build our own strength as well as to secure a healthy future for our planet when we can give ourselves to the commitment that all people should be loved and cared for, that all children should be given every possible assistance as they grow, that all should be fed and clothed and adequately housed, that the human spirit should nowhere be shackled by poverty, exploitation, oppression, or prejudice.

As we begin to see ourselves as intimately connected with all of life, we can no longer be a separate self, alienated from the fate of the whole. We begin to feel the needs of all beings as our own. We see that as long as there is war and hunger, our hearts will not be completely at rest. We feel the life forms of the planet not as resources merely for our use, but as members of our own family. We feel the fate of the rivers, the forests, the plants, and the animals as taking place within the ever-expanding circle of our consciousness.

In our desire to be a part of the love and the healing that is awakening in these times, we don't have to pressure ourselves to try to find our particular path of service. All that is needed is the desire to be of use, and our true service will emerge in its own time and in its own natural way.

Social Action as the Way of Love

A mass of fear has been passed on from generation to generation, sapping our strength and causing us to mistrust and do violence to one another and ourselves. It can be seen not only in war, but also in the preoccupation with war that leads nations to arm against one another and to drain the planet of precious resources.

But at the same time there is something life affirming and eternal that is always with us. There is love, there is a web of light and healing that is spun around this troubled Earth. If we are to make peace in our world, our families, our professions, and our lives, we must activate our healing powers by choosing love over fear.

It is tempting to become so absorbed in external problems that we lose touch with our own inner peace. If we want our lives to be a vehicle for the kind of world for which we pray, we need to keep our hearts open, even when we take a stand in protest. We may disagree most fervently, but we need never become hardened.

When the heart shuts down, we isolate ourselves from the world. When we protest out of fear, we bring as our message not more harmony but more fear. And we ourselves suffer from the very disease that we seek to cure.

If we wish to strengthen our beautiful and wounded world, we must take a stand on behalf of all humanity. Then we can express the kind of power that has been represented by such people as Martin Luther King, Jr., and Mahatma Gandhi. They stood for, spoke for, and lived for peace. They saw the darkness, they saw what must change for the human spirit to take its next step, but their protest was not based in fear. They were willing to go to jail if need be, to suffer, to be treated with cruelty, but they knew they had to live with their hearts open, or they would only add to the burden of hatred and violence already active in the world.

We need never let our aversion to what others are doing get in the way of our love and acceptance of them. For when we are no longer against anyone, but are taking a stand for all, then we become truly effective peacemakers. Our life becomes a statement that the real enemy is the fear that clouds the human heart, and not the person who is acting out that fear.

Balance

*U*p until now, the spiritual journey has primarily been undertaken by isolated individuals. But now it is becoming increasingly apparent that the liberation of the human soul is a shared undertaking. It is something our hearts are doing together. There can ultimately be no independent salvation; we cannot find our true liberation in isolation from one another.

Throughout history, many who tried to live the spiritual life felt a need to be separated from their brothers and sisters. The world seemed to be a source of evil and temptation, something to be denied and transcended. In order for them to negate the Earth with all of her richness and beauty, and to live outside of the community of their fellow human beings, they had to leave a part of themselves unfulfilled.

In the past, many seekers were advised to renounce the world and the pleasures of the flesh, but now the human heart is beginning to awaken into the realization that all of Creation is an act of love, sacred and precious. Many of us are beginning to understand that the world is to be loved, not dismissed. The body is to be respected and enjoyed, not condemned. The suffering of the world is to be healed, not rationalized. The environment is to be conserved and protected, not abused. Animals are to be our neighbors and friends, not exploited as if they were mere objects. And people are to be served and cherished, not forgotten.

During this transitional time, the inner spiritual journey is gradually coming into balance with the outer worldly journey. We are learning how connected we are to the one heart. We are discovering that we are agents of the shared purpose by which the human soul is becoming free.

Those of us who are finding in ourselves a peace and wisdom that belong to all of life are forerunners of the light to come. We are pioneers, forging the pathways across which humanity will travel in the days yet to be.

Whatever role we find ourselves playing on the human stage, we are today being given an extraordinary opportunity: to work together to help to establish the experience of love deep within the consciousness of the human heart.

To contact John Robbins, to receive information about the nonprofit EarthSave International, which he founded, and/or to receive information about his workshops, retreats, river rafting trips, lectures, special events, and other public appearances, write:

John Robbins
c/o EarthSave International
P.O. Box 68
Santa Cruz, CA 95062

To contact Ann Mortifee, to receive information about ordering her cassettes and CDs, and/or to receive information about her concerts, workshops, lectures, special events, and other public appearances, write:

Ann Mortifee
c/o Jabula Records
P.O. Box 91699
West Vancouver, B.C.
Canada V7V 3P3